Life's Instruction Book
FOR WOMEN

by Barbara Gray

Published in Marietta, Georgia by Barbara Gray Proactives.
399 Old Canton Road, Marietta, Georgia 30068.

Typography by Royal Printing, Atlanta, Georgia
Back cover photograph by Head Shots (404) 237-6919

ISBN 0-9637784-0-4

Printed by Vaughan Printing
Nashville, Tennessee

To my best friends who have encouraged me and put up with me. Anne, Penny, Mary Charles, Ellen, Cheryl, Melissa, Dianne, Claudia, Gayle, Johnnie, Kelly, Luis, Joseph, Nan, David, Carol, and Sally. And to my son Lane who awoke me from my forty year sleep when he said, "Don't you get tired getting dumped on?"

Helpful Instructions for Daily Life

1. Celebrate being a woman! You have so much to cheer.

2. Smoking causes little lines above your top lip that make you look older. If you won't give it up for health, give it up for vanity.

3. To thine own self be true- but still color your hair.

4 . Walk three miles every day.

5 . Don't let your material possessions trap you in a dull life of hoarding and dusting.

6 . Expand your vocabulary daily. Choose the words to describe your emotions carefully.

7. Banish your prejudices.

8. Find happiness in helping others. Take your eyes off yourself.

9. Don't buy cheap toilet paper. White is better than colored.

10. Learn how to invest your money. Study, study, study.

11. Eat pasta and steam your veggies.

12. Smell puppy breath-one of life's greatest pleasures.

13. Fat is not a feminist issue.

14. How to tell if you're a doormat? His footprints are smashing your feelings.

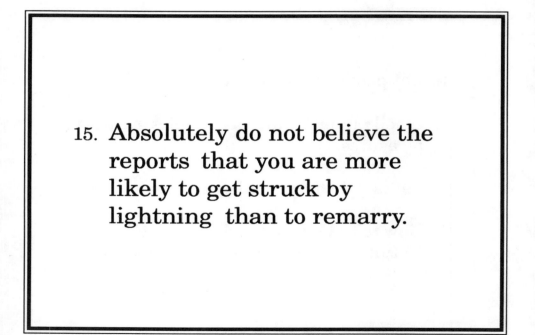

15. Absolutely do not believe the reports that you are more likely to get struck by lightning than to remarry.

16. Teach your son to respect women.

17. Teach your daughters to love and respect themselves.

18. Take a CPR class.

19. Sometimes women do need to think like a man.

20. Report sexual abuse. Stand up for your rights.

21. Hold up your head and you'll stop crying.

22. If you have to put it on a credit card, you probably don't need it. Check the interest rate.

23. Never admit you can type in a job interview.

24. Don't stay married to a man you hate because you're too lazy to work.

25. Put out hummingbird feeders. They're the only birds that can fly backwards.

26. Learn to be flexible like hummingbirds.

27. Make sure there is a designated driver or volunteer to be one.

28. Have at least one skirted table. They're so feminine.

29. Develop your own taste in dressing. Viewing the dresses at the Oscars confirms that you can't buy good taste.

30. Live passionately. Run through piles of leaves, make huge cannonball splashes in the pool, and hit the slopes like an Olympian.

31. Eat popcorn. It's filling and low calorie.

32. Show your power in a group of men by taking out the leader.

33. Pay more attention to details.

34. Remember the thrill of new school supplies each fall? Relive that feeling when you buy things that express you.

35. Reread your teenage diary.

36. Be as wide-eyed as a kitten but as cautious as a leopard.

37. If you lose weight, give away
your fat clothes to show that
you don't intend to wear them.

38. Don't get bogged down in coupons. You'll notice it's never for things like lettuce, broccoli and fruits. It's always some prepackaged fluff.

39. Try to do away with other forms of fluff.

40. Find a woman compelled to vacuum behind her furniture every week and take her to an analyst.

41. Give yourself an Oscar if you can act interested in what a boring man says all night.

42. Go to your class reunion even if you have to go alone.

43. Eat fruits and vegetables because they are rich in vitamins and water.

44. Stick with traditionals: spectator shoes, black velvet dresses, beige raincoats and plaids.

45. Models in the magazines are photographed with special lenses. Don't compare yourself with them.

46. Dancing makes you happy and makes you lose weight.

47. Don't let people call you aggressive when you're assertive.

48. If you must drink coffee, try flavored.

49. Eliminate one of life's most helpless feelings. Put a magnetic key holder (with car keys) under your car.

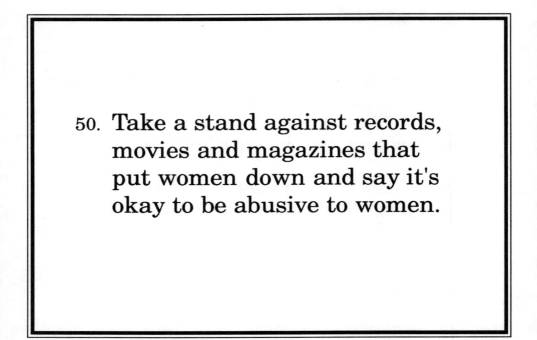

50. Take a stand against records, movies and magazines that put women down and say it's okay to be abusive to women.

51. Scoff at the idea that women aren't good at science and math.

52. Eat alone anywhere you want. Don't feel weird about being alone.

53. Go to a financial planner.

54. Wear sexy underwear with your business clothes.

55. Give blood as often as you can.

56. Always validate people by speaking to them.

57. Vote informed.

58. Set your goals so that you can't accomplish them in your lifetime.

59. Turn on lots of lights during dreary winter months to banish the blues.

60. Buy purses proportionate to your size.

61. Give away clothes you haven't worn in two years.

62. Buy a bouquet of flowers for yourself. Who better?

63. Check out solicitors for charities over the phone. Better yet, give directly.

64. Ask what everyone is wearing to the party and then wear something totally different.

65. Develop your own good taste.

66. Lose weight to show you have control over your life.

67. Be a lady like Audrey Hepburn and an individualist like Katherine Hepburn.

68. Do lipo suction on the tongues of people who call you little lady or my old lady.

69. Think of all the advantages you have being a woman- we rarely go bald, we have an extra layer of fat so we don't get as cold, and we're hotter in the mornings when it really counts.

70. Always wear red on gloomy days.

71. Don't nag.

72. Ladies never use profanity.

73. They also drink their beer in a glass.

74. Buy good accessories for your clothes.

75. Always put a note in Christmas cards.

76. Listen to your children when they are young or they won't listen to you when they are older.

77. Let your daughter have her wedding her way.

78. Dress to show how you want to feel.

79. No whining. Be shining.

80. If something embarrassing happens that you will laugh about later, go ahead and laugh about it now.

81. Find out which colors look best on you. You will get more compliments when you wear them.

82. Banish the words, shoulda, coulda, woulda. They are all past excuses.

83. Fix things around your house yourself. It will make you feel independent.

84. Buy a chain saw and you will really feel independent.

85. Talk to older women. Ask their advice.

86. Diamonds and endorphins are a girl's best friend.

87. Be proud if you are a grandmother.

88. Better to live in a small house and be happy than live in a big house with someone you hate.

89. Eyebrows plucked too much when you're young won't grow back when you are older.

90. Men love women in hats.

91. Revolt against paying more to have your blouse laundered than his shirt. Or wear men's shirts.

92. Have a mammogram regularly.

93. Always have a good book started in your purse in case you have to wait somewhere.

94. Never excuse rude behavior.

95. Take responsibility for not catching AIDS.

96. Keep your girlfriends' secrets.

97. Have fun dressing like a character.
    Shop vintage shops.

98. Treat yourself special, because you are,
    and who knows that better?

99. Being jealous of anyone is wasted energy. You don't know the truth about their life, only yours.

100. Read about and model yourself after the goddesses in mythology. They were brave, bold and powerful.

101. Have a Self Day once a month.

102. Awake from the lifetime of sleep you've been in.

103. Have the presence of a goddess.

104. Set your own stage.

105. Be willing to reveal yourself to the right people.

106. If you really want to talk to someone, don't hesitate because they haven't called you lately. Do what makes you feel good.

107. Hair is a woman's shining glory, so don't neglect yours.

108. Ask questions of everyone you meet. They'll love you for it and you'll learn so much.

109. Is what you do because your mother always did it, or is it the right way to do?

110. Write your autobiography.

111. Remember the other golden rule. The one who has the gold, rules.

112. Wearing shoes that hurt your feet will show in your face.

113. Speak slowly with confidence.

114. Putting lipstick on fuller than your lips always shows.

115. Treat yourself to a vacation.

116. Avoid negative people like a zit on the end of your nose.

117. Simplify, simplify.

118. Be a great listener.

119. Thank God you are a woman born in America.

120. Vote for women candidates if they are equally qualified and will represent their constituents better than their opponents.

121. Speak to everyone around you.

122. Write your own songs, "To All The Men I've Ever Known".

123. Read the business section of the newspaper.

124. Have a good stereo system.

125. A terry cloth robe can go a long way toward making you cozy.

126. Weed negative people out of your life.

127. Memorize famous quotations.

128. Your period always starts the day you wear white pants.

Inner Thinking

Inner Thinking

All of our thinking comes from a source of inner thinking or outer thinking. This labeling is different than calling thought either positive or negative because it is the source of our thinking. The ultimate decision of whether we take actions on our thoughts should be based on whether it came from inner thinking, inspired by the spirit of God, or outer thinking, based on the events in our lives or our current emotions.

When we were born, God gave us our specific talents and abilities, our true worth, which does not vary, and an inner spirit which is inspired by God and knows only Truth. After we were born, we developed our own thinking. It is influenced by what is around us and the people around us, the events which happened to us, and our emotions. From our other thinking grew our false self which added fear, guilt, anger, self-pity and self-righteousness to our lives. If we let these negative emotions control our lives or even the positive emotions, then we have no control over our lives.

If you take every thought, every action, every principle and make it follow the guidelines of inner thinking, you will never make bad decisions, experience hurtful emotions and feelings. God has given us the power through knowing our inner-self, which is enlightened by His perfect wisdom, to always seek the Truth and our life's fulfillment.

When we hear the words, "giving up ourself," we think that we are going to lose ourself. But the outer self has grown since you were born. The outer self is the source of the bad things you think you are because of what your parents either said to you or did to you . Your interpretation of the things that happened to you was good or bad, not what actually happened to you.

As a child we competed in various contests. We suffered because we did not win and many of us felt defeated because we did not know we are to learn from our defeats. We didn't realize that we only had to be our best. We've made all of life a contest where we thought our happiness depended on winning all these contests. We rely on our outer thinking rather than inner thinking.

We set our expectations according to the thinking of our outer false self. Our worth has never been determined by the contests we have won or lost. Still, we are always putting our lives in contests. We have a list of wants, people and events we want to control, promises we think life has made to us.

Look at what outer thinking does to our lives. We worry about the future because we don't know that our inner self has the power it needs to understand and deal with the situation. The things that happen to us are only good or bad depending on our reaction to them.

Secondly, we're afraid to seek our true inner self because we have become so accustomed to our false thinking. How could we not revere our inner self? It's source of inspiration is God and as the inner self continuously corrects itself, it becomes closer to the Father.

Lastly, outer thinking has convinced us that our emotions control us. We are never to feel bad. Let me say it again- we are never to feel bad. How does this work? Do you think God ever feels depressed? Of course not, and since we have the Spirit of God within us, He has given us the power through our emotions not over our emotions.

So why do we have emotions? They operate for the same reason we have nerve endings all over our bodies. When we touch something hot, our nerve endings alert us to danger. Our emotions are to act as indicators. Our emotions are not to make us feel good or bad. They are to be indicators. They are signal lights that come on to help us know in our moment by moment efforts to be our real self, that we are relying on outer thinking rather than inner thinking.

How will life be when you change to inner thinking? First, all of our actions will be activated from within rather than directed from the ideas of the outer world or our outer self. Second, you will know your decisions are right because the Truth never varies or lies. Third, the weaknesses you have acquired are not really you. They lie about your lack of power, your need to control, what it takes to make you happy, and what it takes to make you succeed.

Lastly inner thinking realizes that no one can help you- not even yourself. We can't rely on others to tell us where to go or what to do. Inner thinking directs your life by letting you perceive the Truth which never changes and is always right.

An inner thinking person is attuned to a life without limits. Events in life become challenges to one's inner thinking. They do not think compulsively. They walk away from problems and feelings that cause suffering. Knowing that they must begin to think differently, inner thinkers take command of their lives and operate from the inner being connected to a higher power, from strength rather than weakness. They live according to understanding and power within.

1. Happiness comes from your inner self. You can be happy all the time.

2. Emotions can be controlled. You are in charge!

3. Listen to the "still quiet voice".

4. Know that you are made in the image of God.

5. Don't feel yourself, be yourself.

6. Take responsibility for your own happiness, you can't find it in another.

7. Make a list of your talents and abilities.

8. You can only be as free as you are willing to be truthful about yourself.

9. Women don't need to act more like men to have more power. They need to use their innate qualities of intuition, creativity, and nurturing.

10. Give up trying to please others. Please yourself by doing what is right.

11. Happiness is not having preconceived ideas of what happiness is.

12. When we stop fearing to uncover what's wrong with us, we'll find out what's right.

13. Being married doesn't mean giving up your inner self.

14. You have to be willing to spend time alone to reveal your inner self.

15. If what you're doing in life isn't working, then do something else. We fail to get new results doing the same old things.

16. Liberation is not the freedom to act like men, it is the freedom to be who you are.

17. Speak the Truth.

18. Be a person achieving your life's purpose- that's the opposite of a woman driven by life.

19. We are not to suffer in life. Change your attitudes towards those things which cause you pain.

20. Quit trying to make everyone like you. You are not seeking Truth or speaking the Truth. If you are following the directions of the inner self, not all people will like you because they hate the Truth.

21. Since we aren't promised anything from life, we can't be disappointed with what we have. Contentment is happiness.

22. You have to have a void before you fill it up. You may have to get more empty than you want to, and have to say I've had more than enough, to get your self to make changes.

23. Detecting weakness instigates rejecting weaknesses.

24. Keep growing through self-correction.

25. Doubt and fear are what make you limited.

26. Live in the present moment by moment.

27. A person with power doesn't have to seek it.
It comes from within.

28. Never seek approval from others.
Be your true self, and you will be
all the person you need to be.

29. You have within you all the answers
to your life's questions.

30. When a woman reveals herself to herself, nothing is hidden in the world.

31. Human beings are not to be dominated by anything on this earth.

Motivational Thoughts

Who Killed Your Dreams?

I wish someone had told the secret to me,

That I could be anything I wanted to be.

The Indians made dream catchers to hang over their heads while they slept. The circle is laced with small twigs or bits of thread to catch the bad dreams. The good dreams pass through the web and would pass down through the feathers and to the sleeper. Some bad dreams are caught and they're destroyed by the first rays of sunlight, while others escape through the center hole.

God gave us all symbolic dream catchers to encircle our heads while we sleep. It is waiting for you. Reclaim your gift!

What happened to your dreams?
They were killed by the people who said:
"No one in our family has ever done that."
"We can't afford that."
"I don't know how you expect to do that."
"I've never heard of that."
"Girls can't do that."

Each of these remarks attacks our self-esteem. We thought our parents knew whether we would fail or succeed. We let wounded people steal our dreams from our dream catchers.

We go through high school and college still clinging to these attitudes. How many times have you said or heard others say

"I was never popular in high school", or "I did not do well in that subject in high school?" They've been out of high school for 20 years and haven't changed their thinking since they got their diploma.

They didn't understand that the commencement address meant new beginning and was a challenge for new beliefs. A national news reporter said on TV that he had to miss his high school reunion. He said, "they didn't miss me because they didn't like me anyhow". His perception of himself had not changed since he was 18 years old.

Take a detached look at your parents. Most of them either couldn't express their love, were emotionally or physically abused, suffered low self-esteem, or they had oppressive parents. Are you going to let someone like that set the standard for your self worth? These wounded people were never able to resolve their problems, so how can you expect them to deal with yours. Are you going to pass along your problems to your children?

Take a minute to look at your life. Are you a person who likes changes or prefers to stay with the same routine? We are striving for improvement, so won't we have to constantly be making changes? Those who falsely think they have reached perfection can't admit they make mistakes. And the rest of us beat ourselves up when we make a mistake because we don't understand that this is the way we learn. Become your true self by being willing to make corrections.

Make some changes in your time schedule. Get up a half hour earlier to read, meditate or exercise. Make changes in your eating habits. Buy different style clothes. Try some new activities. If you say you don't have time, stop watching so much TV and reading negative or non-thought provoking materials. Try to do everything differently.

1. Why worry when you can pray?

2. Listen to motivational tapes.

3. Read biographies about ordinary women who led extraordinary lives.

4. Be pro-active, which means taking responsibility for your life.

5. Keep a journal of your purposes in life- long term, short term and daily.

6. Listen to classical music to stimulate your subconscious.

7. Make your own fortunes.

8. When you know your purpose, risk it all, and you will be happy.

9. Tackle jobs you thought were impossible and gain strength from doing them.

10. Get over Learned Helplessness.

11. Don't buy things to feel happy. Change your state by thinking happy thoughts or remembering happy events.

12. Get your life together and you'll send out great vibes that will attract positive people.

13. Believe in yourself.

14. Spend lots more time in the library and bookstores.

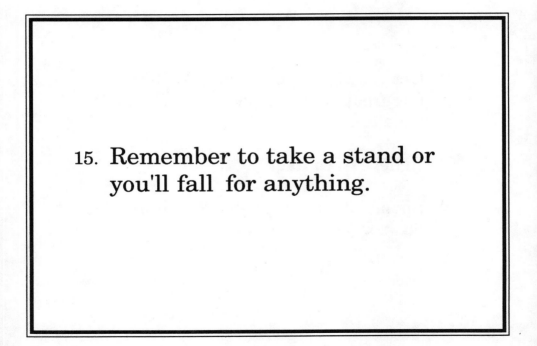

15. Remember to take a stand or you'll fall for anything.

16. Model the duck in the pond who stays calm on top and paddles like hell below.

17. 95% of the way we act and think is based on our self-image.

18. Remember to say two positives before you present your negative.

19. Ideas are nothing without action.

20. If you can't take a vacation, take a vacation in your mind.

21. Read books on time management.

22. Learn to relax, relax, relax.

23. Have a garden. They're wonderful places to think.

24. Take time to meditate. Communicate with God through your subconscious mind. Let Him know your desires and He will help you achieve them.

25. Forget the excuse, "I'm just a woman".

26. Be extremely persistent. All great people have this quality and it has paid off. Your reward could be behind your next efforts.

27. Remember, if you're not growing, you're dead.

28. Be a limitless person.

29. Successful women aren't afraid to wear red lipstick.

30. Break with traditional roles. Stand out!

31. To gain more power, practice lowering your voice. Whiney women never get anywhere.

32. You will reap what you sow.

33. Talk to yourself only in positive terms.

34. Be glad if you are mostly right brained which makes you creative and able to deal with relationships.

35. Find a successful mentor.

36. Before you can get anything different out of this life, you must first do things differently.

37. Worry focuses on the future and will make you inactive. ***Live in the moment!***

38. Use your forebrain (conscious mind) to select, evaluate, and form judgments. Then pass this information on to your sub-conscious, which will tell you how to put it into action.

40. The only person you can really count on is your inner self.

41. Get to the point when you talk.

42. Celebrate LIFE!

43. The past will not guide you in the future.

44. Keep a journal by your bed. Your subconscious is active during the night and you will awaken to your best inspirations.

45. It takes very few letters to affect sponsors. Let them know you don't like the garbage on TV.

46. Write down your thoughts the minute they come to you, or they'll be gone forever.

47. Look at problems as opportunities.

48. Turn your brain off at night by playing a tape of soft music.

49. Practice everyday for success by doing things differently so you will be ready for change.

50. Find a private think tank in your home where you feel comfortable and creative.

51. If you want others to change their opinions about you, change your opinion about yourself.

52. Remember how to daydream. It's the stuff goals are made of.

53. Remember to pray often.

54. Also, be glad that you can use your left brain and be logical.

55. Be PROACTIVE!

56. Celebrate being a woman! You have so much to celebrate.

57. Remember how you were at six- not afraid to try anything and unconcerned what others thought of you.

58. Be more than you ever thought possible.

59. Quit letting men abuse you and your children. You do not need someone who hurts you.

60. Use your God given nurturing ability in the management field.

61. Do what you passionately love and care about and you will be successful.

Single Women

1. Instead of believing a man when he says "I'll call you", take his phone number and tell him you'll call him, if you really plan to.

2. Men who aren't listed in the phone book or won't give you their home phone number are married.

3. Pick your purpose in life, risk it all, and you will be happy.

4. Forget the idea that you will love only one man.

5. Don't wait for a man to pick you out, choose the one you want.

6. A man who tries to get you to drink too much is trying to lower your defenses. Set limits and retain dignity.

7. Let your friends know if you're looking for a new man. It pays to advertise.

8. Spend a lot of time with each other's children before you marry. It's a package deal.

9. Be kind to your friends. They'll be there after he's come and gone.

10. Hang around some married couples and you'll be glad you're single. As a matter of fact, you'll love it.

11. Keep a man guessing by not accounting for every minute of your time.

12. Decide which things are negotiable and which things are not negotiable.

13. Women involved with a married man lack self-esteem or they wouldn't put up with a part time relationship. You are worth more.

14. You get back what you send out. So if you wear sexy clothes to attract a man, you'll get a man whose brains are below his belt and he won't appreciate you.

15. You can get a credit history on anyone. Have it done before you marry. Some men live off divorcees and widows.

16. Stop wasting your life being a Delta Dawn.

17. Most married men will stay with their wives.

18. Make new family traditions after the divorce. Let your children know you are still a family.

19. Stay away from men who are only interested in you for your looks. If you have a mastectomy or get wrinkles, they will leave you.

21. Before you marry, think about being stranded on an island with him and make sure he's the one you want to talk to everyday.

22. Asking a man what he does for a living first thing is out.

23. You don't have to let strangers hold you too tight on the dance floor.

24. It's okay to meet a man through a personal ad, but if he wants to meet you at the Waffle House, skip it.

25. Men who come on too fast leave as fast as they came.

26. Forget the man in white armor- by now he's the tin man.

27. Be convinced you are not going to change him after you marry.

28. Don't turn down a man who asks you to dance. It's not a marriage contract.

29. Stay away from men still tied to their ex-wives or girlfriends.

30. Talking about your cat on dates makes you sound like an old maid.

31. Never, never, never wait by the phone for a man. If he wants to call you, he'll call back.

32. If a man doesn't call, don't make excuses for him.

33. Don't drop out of sight because you have a new boyfriend.

34. Go by what a man does rather than what he says.

35. Snide remarks about your ex will bore people, and they'll wonder why you were so dumb to marry him.

36. Talk to a man's first wife before you marry him. Only believe half of what she says, but really listen to the other half.

37. Ask men who keep persisting after you have said no, which part they do not understand.

38. Talk to your friends who have gotten a divorce and find out if the judge was fair. If he wasn't, vote him out to protect your daughters and other women.

39. You'll look back and laugh at most of the men you cried over so why not laugh over them now.

40. Take responsibility and don't expect your attorney to look after you financially.

41. Feeling jealous of his new life or girl friend is a waste of time. You know all too well what he's really like.

42. Watch how a man treats children and dogs.

43. Watch the way a man treats his mother. He'll probably treat you the same way.

44. Stay away from men who don't like women.

45. Listen to what a man tells you when you first meet him. They are usually honest about their faults.

46. Be honest to your girlfriends about your man's bad behavior. If not, then you're lying to yourself.

47. Find a man who'll be your friend and lover.

48. No other person in the world will ever be just like you, so don't let a man compare you to his dead wife or mother.

49. Figure out what the other person's motive is.

50. When you're sad because you don't have a man around, REMEMBER:

Whiskers in the sink.

Little dark body hairs in your bed.

Belches and farts.

Amnesia on garbage day.

Having ESPN on all your TV stations.

Riding 400 miles having to listen to football games all the way.

Dead silence after you've spent 20 minutes pouring out your heart to someone who has shut down his emotions.

Having someone with bad breath at 6 a.m. wanting sex.

51. Always have a plan B, especially if you're dealing with a man.

52. A man who can't dance too well hasn't hung around bars too long and might be a good partner.

53. If you are determined to get married, set goals of meeting five or ten men a month.

54. If your girlfriend tries to break pre-arranged plans with you because a man just called, tell her, "no, it's not all-right".

55. Men come and go, but your children are always yours, so treat them like the precious beings they are.

56. Sometimes you feel like a hockey team goalie. Everyone is hitting the puck at you as hard as they can, and if you get out of your little cage, they try to knock you down. Remember, you have the biggest stick, the most padding and you return the puck a lot more than they get it through.

57. The sooner you quit being naive, the sooner people will not be able to take advantage of you.

58. When a man does wrong, don't make excuses for him.

59. Make sure he has a sense of humor.

60. Sleep with a man who likes to spoon.

61. Call on your friends when you need help. Single women need an extremely strong support group.

62. Say "I am single". Don't call yourself divorced. Divorce is an event, not a state of being.

63. Check how marriage might affect your social security benefits.

64. Have a list of requirements for the men you date. If they do not measure up, drop them.

65. No law requires you to date only one man at a time.

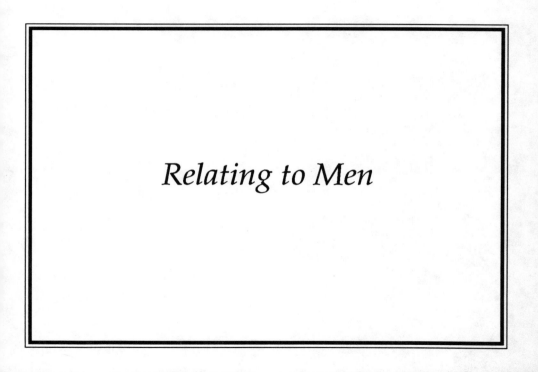

Relating to Men

1. Treat a short man like the tall man he is on the inside.

2. A man who brags about his car too much doesn't have his values in the right order.

3. Expect a man to show up when you see the whites of his eyes.

4. Turn a man into a raging bull, shave with his razor.

5. Stay away from men who won't ride with a woman driver.

6. Men are fascinated with polished fingernails and toenails.

7. Overcome the fear of men by picturing them as little boys standing in their underwear.

8. Men are competitive. They will want you more if someone else does. If they are afraid of the competition, they have low self-esteem anyhow.

9. Become a super intellect by figuring out why men like to buy black vinyl and leather couches. And why they always like red to go with it.

10. Men think that if you invite them to your house, it means for stay-over. Make it clear upfront what you intend.

11. Give up understanding the mind of man when you don't even know why he has nipples.

12. Men always jingle the money in their pockets rather than spend it on the calls they promised to make.

13. What's more fun than male bashing? Nothing!

14. If all the good men are taken, why do their wives say they will never marry after they get rid of this one?

15. God's remark after creating man: "I can do better than that."

16. Will Rogers said "I never met a man I didn't like." Can you believe that!

17. Bald headed men are overly sensitive about hair loss, so always treat them nice.

18. Very few men are really handsome, and those that are have so many women after them, they're ruined for life.

19. Be sensitive, men have feelings too.

20. Men who like to garden aren't as exciting as some men, but they're more planted.

21. A good man is hard to find. And a hard man is good to find.

22. Understand why short men act on the defensive.

23. Everyone likes a compliment, so if you want to talk to a man, find something you admire.

24. Be kind to ugly men. They're some mother's baby boy.

25. A man who isn't pleased with the way you look in the mornings places too much value on the superficial.

26. Men are good for only two things-moving heavy furniture and occasionally he's good for the other.

27. You know nature has a great sense of humor because women are always horny during their periods.

28. Hide his remote control.

29. The solution to the fragile male ego, let them dry up and die.

30. You can tell everyone your news, but until you tell it to your mate, you haven't told it.

The movie "Separate but Equal" chronicled the desegrega-
tion of the school systems during the 50's. Thurgood
Marshall cited a test before the Supreme Court where black
children were asked to decide which doll was better, the
black doll or the white doll. Every black child said the white
doll was better. Until recently, if a test were given to me, but
asking, "which is better, the male doll or the female doll?" I
would have chosen the male doll.

Men generally appeared to be more in control of their
lives, and to have fewer boundaries. I don't admire males
more than females, but they have always seemed to have
the advantage. The last time I thought I had the power, to

be just what I wanted to be, was in the first grade where I was the leader on the playground. What happened to that bold and confident five year old?

My story is not to say that I've had an unusual life, but it is to say that like most women, something happened to that little girl that kept her from being the most she could be.

Recently, a simple question by a career counselor asking, "what kind of job have you always wanted?" led me to make the most profound changes in my life. I thought my divorce in 1980, which took away my financial security, self-esteem and confidence, had caused me to make radical changes. But the decision to become proactive in my life revealed an inner self that would cause me to change my whole being.

It is when you discover your purpose in life, molded and influenced by the events in your life, that you begin to change. Our bodies have all the necessary makings of either a man or woman. An added or minus chromosome, fewer or more hormones could have made me go either way. Whether I became male or female wasn't the important thing, it was knowing that I had an inner self, life-lined to the Spirit of God.

Taking time to study what makes us act and do, led to the following insights.

I learned that I am becoming more of an inner thinker. And when I have chosen inner thinking, life has succeeded and when I chose outer thinking, life was hard and depressing. On the other hand, my harried activities have kept me from thinking. Guilt comes from knowing that you possess creative thinking abilities and repress them from fear or not wanting to take responsibility for putting them into action. How can you expect others to have faith in you, if you don't have faith in yourself?

The greatest freedom comes when you see yourself as a set of one, a unique individual who will never be duplicated, someone revealed impossible for comparison. There are no average people. How can we be categorized when there are so many facets to our being. Can you say Madonna is an above average American because of the money she makes, and classify a woman who has unselfishly devoted her life to helping babies with aids as a below average American because she is poor? How can there be average people when there is no standard, no measure to compare them: Who has our uniqueness, our spirit?

My spirit shouted, free, free at last when I saw "past mistakes" as learning processes where I did the best I could at the time. Moving through the fear of failures criticism creates the "I am". Who has the right to judge me? I don't have to run as fast, be as pretty, dress as nice, be as smart as anyone else.

When my thinking came from my inner self, I began to speak the Truth, not what was expected or what others would like to hear. The Truth was the only measure.

Recognizing your emotions became okay. They are to drive you toward your purpose in life. The dream you have stays a dream until you passionately decide to take some action. And then when your emotions ping or pang, you know it is to help you focus on your goal.

When I realized that I will always be me, I began to love me. Everything I have ever done, thought or sensed is stored in my brain. But I can change these internal representations by changing my attitude about what has happened. They are not me. My value was set when I was born, and I will never be worth more or less than I have always been.

Order Form

Want additional copies of this book? Life's Instruction Book for Women makes a great gift for friends.

Yes, I want to order additional copies of Life's Instruction Book for Women because my friend took mine or I want to give copies to all my friends.

Each book $5.95. Please add $2 per book for postage and handling. Georgia residents must include 5% state sales tax. (Canadian order must be accompanied by postal money order in U.S. funds.) Allow 30 days for delivery. Send check payable to:

BARBARA GRAY PROACTIVES,
399 Old Canton Road, Marietta, Georgia 30068